REBECCA
LOBO

BY RICHARD RAMBECK

(Photo on front cover)

Rebecca Lobo during New York's 65–57 WNBA victory over Phoenix Mercury. June 19, 1997.

(Photo on previous pages)

Rebecca Lobo leads the team off the bench at the end of their 96–79 victory over Australia in women's Olympic Basketball. From left are Lobo, Katy Steding, Venus Lacey, and Dawn Staley. July 27, 1996.

GRAPHIC DESIGN
Robert A. Honey, Seattle

PHOTO RESEARCH
James R. Rothaus, James R. Rothaus & Associates

ELECTRONIC PRE-PRESS PRODUCTION
Robert E. Bonaker, Graphic Design & Consulting Co.

PHOTOGRAPHY
All photos by Associated Press AP

Printed in the United States of America.

Library of Congress Cataloging-in-Publication Data
Rambeck, Richard
Rebecca Lobo / by Richard Rambeck
p. cm.
Summary: Presents a biography of the star center of the WNBA's New York Liberty whose career highlights include winning the 1996 Olympic gold medal.
ISBN 1-56766-524-1 (library : reinforced : alk. paper)

1. Lobo, Rebecca — Juvenile literature.
2. Women basketball players—United States—Biography—Juvenile literature.
[1. Lobo, Rebecca. 2. Women basketball players. 3. Basketball players. 4. Women—Biography] I. Title
GV884.L6R36 1998 97-52771
796.323'092 — dc21 CIP
[B] AC

CONTENTS

Lobo pulls in a rebound during the game against Tennessee at Storrs, Connecticut on January 16, 1995.

It wasn't going to be easy for Rebecca Lobo, or for her teammates on the U.S. Olympic women's basketball team. Lobo was the youngest player on the team that competed in the 1996 Olympics in Atlanta. She was also probably the most famous. Before joining the Olympic squad, Lobo led the University of Connecticut (UConn) Huskies to the NCAA women's college basketball title in 1995. She topped the Huskies in scoring (17.1 points per game), rebounding (9.8 a game), and blocked shots (3.5) during the 1994–95 season. UConn played 35 games that season; the Huskies won all 35.

ON TOP FOR GOOD

No team—Men's or women's—in NCAA history had ever won that many games in a season. UConn, however, nearly wound up 34–1. In the title game against Tennessee, the Huskies struggled for most of the game. UConn trailed 38–32 at halftime. In the second half, the two teams traded the lead back and forth. Finally, the Huskies went on top for good with less than two minutes left to play. Behind Lobo's game–high 17 points, UConn won 70–64. To no one's surprise, Lobo was named the most outstanding player of the NCAA tournament.

Lobo displays her trophy after being named national player of the year in women's basketball by the Associated Press. March 31, 1995 in Minneapolis.

LOBO BECOMES FAMOUS

UConn and Lobo did more than win the NCAA title in 1995; they attracted a lot of attention to women's basketball. In fact, no women's team had ever received the kind of attention UConn did. Lobo, a graceful, 6–foot–4 forward, was the most popular UConn player. She appeared on "Late Night with David Letterman." She went jogging with President Bill Clinton. Her hometown, Southwick, Massachusetts, named a street after her: Rebecca Lobo Way. One day she was getting a haircut. As soon as she got out of the chair, someone ran into the salon and scooped up her hair and put it in a bag.

8

LOBO'S CAREER GROWS

Lobo's college career ended with the title game victory over Tennessee. During her four years at UConn, Lobo averaged 16.9 points per game. She was named women's national college player of the year after her senior season. She was selected to the U.S. Olympic team, which spent a year playing exhibition games to prepare for the Summer Games in Atlanta. Lobo was 21 years old when she joined the Olympic team. Most of her teammates were much older. Almost all of them had been playing for years on professional teams in other countries.

"ROOKIE"

It didn't take long for Lobo's Olympic teammates to give her a nickname. They called the most recent NCAA player of the year "Rookie." It wasn't an easy situation for the team. Lobo might have been the best-known member of the team, but she was not the best player by a long shot, especially at first. "It was

11

difficult for her," said U.S. coach Tara VanDerveer. "It was also hard on the rest of the team because they've been playing overseas and people hadn't heard about them." But people had heard about Lobo, who was facing stiff competition in practice every day.

Lobo of the New York Liberty and Los Angeles Sparks' Lisa Leslie go after the ball at New York's Madison Square Garden. August 5, 1997.

READY TO LEARN

She was playing against players as big or bigger and as quick or quicker than she was," VanDerveer said. Instead of being afraid of the challenge she faced, Lobo enjoyed it. She knew what her role on the team was. She didn't have to be a star, just a player who worked hard. "I don't have to try to be the leading scorer and the leading rebounder," she said. "I'm going in ready to learn and hoping to contribute. I know it's very different from the past four years in college, but it's still basketball. I'm very fortunate to be a part of this team."

Lobo faces off against her former teammate Jamelle Elliot during an exibition game between UConn and USA National Team. November 5, 1995.

A GOOD TEAMMATE

Lobo proved to be a good teammate. She practiced hard, kept her mouth shut, and tried to fit in. "She had a lot of growing up to do and she's been forced to do it really fast. To her credit, she's doing it," said Teresa Edwards, a 32–year–old guard who was playing on her fourth Olympic team. The Olympic squad spent the fall of 1995 and the winter of 1996 playing U.S. college teams from all over the country. The Olympians were just too good for the college teams—way too good. The Olympic squad won most of the games by at least 40 points.

THE OLYMPICS

Once the Olympic tournament started, the United States continued to roll to easy victories. In five first–round games, the Americans won all five and averaged more than 100 points while giving up only 68. The United States beat Japan 108–93 in the quarterfinals and then defeated Australia 93–71 in the semifinals. In the gold medal game, Teresa Edwards and forward Lisa Leslie led the Americans to a 111–87 victory over Brazil. Every U.S. player scored in the game. The U.S. men's basketball squad was called the "Dream Team," but the women proved to be just as much of a dream.

Lobo and Lisa Leslie celebrate their 101–84 win over Cuba at Morehouse College in Atlanta, July 21, 1996.

A NEW CHALLENGE

After the Olympics, Lobo faced a new challenge. She agreed to play in a new professional league in the United States, the Women's National Basketball Association. Several times in the past, professional basketball leagues for women had failed in the United States. That's why most of Lobo's Olympic teammates played in leagues in other countries. The WNBA, though, was different from those other failed leagues. For one thing, it had the backing of the NBA, the National Basketball Association. In addition, all WNBA teams played in large NBA arenas, and the league had an excellent TV contract.

Lobo has the ball knocked away from her by Sacramento Monarchs Corissa Yasen during the first half at New York's Madison Square Garden. July 15, 1997.

We're excited," Lobo said of the women who played in the WNBA's first season, in the summer of 1997. "It's not just about us. It's about women being in TV commercials for professional leagues. It's about so much energy and enthusiasm for the start of this league." Lobo's team, the New York Liberty, began the season with seven victories in a row. That continued a remarkable streak for Lobo. UConn won the last 35 games she played. The Olympic team won all 60 games it played. When the Liberty's streak reached seven, Lobo's own winning streak totaled 102.

FIRST TIME LOSSES

Finally, for the first time in more than three years, she played on the losing side in a game. The Liberty went on to post a 17–11 record and finish second in its division behind Houston. Lobo played all 28 games for the Liberty. She averaged 12.4 points and 7.3 rebounds per game, which was fifth best in the league. Lobo also blocked 1.82 shots per game, the fourth highest average in the WNBA. She had some outstanding games. Lobo had 27 points, 9 rebounds, and 5 blocked shots in a win over Utah. She scored 20 and grabbed 7 rebounds as the Liberty beat Cleveland.

Lobo works at getting past Utah Starzz center Elena Baranova for a shot during the first half of their game in Salt Lake City, Utah.
August 19, 1997.

A "ROOKIE" NO MORE

New York faced Phoenix in one WNBA semifinal game. Lobo was at her best. She led the team with 16 points and 9 rebounds as New York won 59–41. Lobo chipped in 4 assists and 3 blocked shots. Lobo also played well in the WNBA title game, scoring 9 points and getting 9 rebounds. Unfortunately, Houston won the game 65–61. After the season, Lobo was named to the WNBA's all–league second team. Rebecca Lobo was a "Rookie" no more. She was a professional basketball player, and a good one. In fact, she was living a childhood dream—sort of.

Lobo goes up for a basket against the Phoenix Mercury at Madison Square Garden. Her team won 78–70 and Lobo got 12 of her 18 points in the second half. August 2, 1997.

When she was eight years old, Lobo wrote a letter to Red Auerbach, president of the Boston Celtics. In the letter, she told Auerbach she wanted to be the first girl to play for the Celtics. Lobo did more than write letters, though. "I started playing basketball at a really young age, and I practiced all the time," she said. Lobo grew up admiring Larry Bird and then David Robinson, center of the San Antonio Spurs. While Lobo didn't wind up playing for the Celtics, she did live up to the standards of her idols, Robinson and Bird. Like them, Lobo won an Olympic gold medal and became a professional basketball player.